Parent's Introduction

We Both Read is the first series of books designed to invite parents and children to share the reading of a story by taking turns reading aloud. This "shared reading" innovation, which was developed with reading education specialists, invites parents to read the more complex text and storyline on the left-hand pages. Then, children can be encouraged to read the right-hand pages, which feature less complex text and storyline, specifically written for the beginning reader.

Reading aloud is one of the most important activities parents can share with their child to assist them in their reading development. However, *We Both Read* goes beyond reading *to* a child and allows parents to share the reading *with* a child. *We Both Read* is so powerful and effective because it combines two key elements in learning: "modeling" (the parent reads) and "doing" (the child reads). The result is not only faster reading development for the child, but a much more enjoyable and enriching experience for both!

You may find it helpful to read the entire book aloud yourself the first time, then invite your child to participate in the second reading. In some books, a few more difficult words will first be introduced in the parent's text, distinguished with **bold lettering**. Pointing out, and even discussing, these words will help familiarize your child with them and help to build your child's vocabulary. Also, note that a "talking parent" icon ⌐ precedes the parent's text and a "talking child" icon ⌐ precedes the child's text.

We encourage you to share and interact with your child as you read the book together. If your child is having difficulty, you might want to mention a few things to help them. "Sounding out" is good, but it will not work with all words. Children can pick up clues about the words they are reading from the story, the context of the sentence, or even the pictures. Some stories have rhyming patterns that might help. It might also help them to touch the words with their finger as they read, to better connect the voice sound and the printed word.

Sharing the *We Both Read* books together will engage you and your child in an interactive adventure in reading! It is a fun and easy way to encourage and help your child to read—and a wonderful way to start them off on a lifetime of reading enjoyment!

We Both Read: Endangered Animals

———————————————————

Text Copyright © 2006 by Elise Forier
Use of photographs provided by Getty Images (Photodisc), Fotosearch, Corel, Digital
Vision, Corbis Photos, Thinkstock Photos, Brand X, and IT Stock Free Photos.
Illustrations Copyright (pgs. 5-6) © by Robert Walters
Illustrations Copyright (pgs. 7-8) © 2006 by Judith Hunt

We Both Read® is a trademark of Treasure Bay, Inc.

Published by Treasure Bay, Inc.
40 Sir Francis Drake Boulevard
San Anselmo, CA 94960 USA

PRINTED IN SINGAPORE

Library of Congress Catalog Card Number: 2005911327

Hardcover ISBN-10: 1-891327-71-2
Hardcover ISBN-13: 978-1-891327-71-1
Paperback ISBN-10: 1-891327-72-0
Paperback ISBN-13: 978-1-891327-72-8

We Both Read® Books
Patent No. 5,957,693

Visit us online at:
www.webothread.com

WE BOTH READ®

Endangered Animals

By Elise Forier

TREASURE BAY

The world is full of animals. Go to a forest, or beach, or even your own back yard, and you will see all kinds of creatures. They are very busy, finding and eating food, building homes, hiding from danger, and taking care of their young.

Animals live almost everywhere—in grass, trees, underwater, even underground and in dark dens.

All animals need food to eat and water to drink. They also need a safe place to live and sleep.

Red squirrel

☍   For some animals, finding food, water and a safe home is very easy.

    This **squirrel** lives in a tree in a park. She drinks from a nearby creek and eats the nuts and fruit that grow in the trees. The park is big and she has lots of space where she can search for food and play. Even if a dog runs after her, she can scamper up a tree trunk and be safe.

Red squirrel

If all the trees in the park were cut down, the **squirrel** would have no home. It would be hard for her to find food. If a dog ran after her, she wouldn't have a place to hide.

Quetzalcoatlus

Megatherium

Tyrannosaurus Rex

When animals cannot find enough food or water or a safe place to live, they often die. When all of one kind of animal dies, we say the animal species is **extinct**.

Long ago, the animals in this picture lived in various parts of the world, but the land, water and air changed and these animals became **extinct**.

Stegosaurus

Mammoth

Triceratops

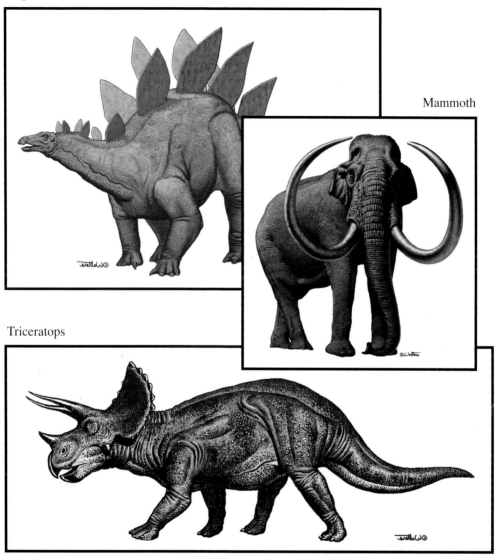

🐾   There are many ways for animals to become **extinct.**
The air can get too cold or hot. Water can dry up. Plants
that the animals eat can die.

An animal that is extinct is gone for all time.

Dodo birds

 Sometimes animals become extinct because people interfere.
Dodo birds lived not so long ago on a faraway island, called Mauritius, near India. Dodos were very gentle birds that could not fly. Since the dodos didn't have any natural predators on their island, the dodos were not frightened by the sailors who arrived in 1505.

Soon more people came on boats with dogs and rats. The **dodos** did not run away from them. The people killed the dodos for food. The rats and dogs ate dodo eggs. The last dodo died in 1681. Dodos are now extinct.

 Today there are many animals all over the world that are in danger of becoming extinct. They are called **endangered** animals. Most of them are dying because the world is changing too fast. New roads and highways may cover their homes. Dangerous pesticides, used to control insects, might poison their food and water. Forests are cut down and then there is nowhere to hide and be safe. Hunters may kill so many of a certain kind of animal that few, or none, are left alive.

Young snow leopard

 It is sad that some animals are **endangered**, but "endangered" is not extinct. If we make sure all endangered animals can find food, water and safe places to live, they may never become extinct.

Giant panda eating bamboo

The place where an animal lives is called its "**habitat**". Many animals live in very unique **habitats**, where they eat certain foods and build special nests.

Giant **pandas** live in the mountains of China where they eat a tall, woody plant called **bamboo**. The bamboo forest is the panda's special **habitat**.

Giant panda

 **Pandas** are endangered because their **habitat** is disappearing. People cut down the **bamboo** forests where they live. Each year, there is less and less of their habitat where the pandas can eat and hide.

Golden lion tamarin

Golden lion tamarins are monkeys that live across the world from pandas in the South American rain forest. Like pandas, tamarins are losing their forest habitat and have become endangered. People cut down the forest to make charcoal and other wood products. They also cut down trees to make room for farms and roads. Every year, the tamarins have fewer trees in which to live and raise their families.

Amazon clearcut forest

There are lots of other wild animals that also need the rain forest trees for their habitat. If all the rain forests are cut down, many of these animals will become extinct.

Siberian tiger

Several different kinds of tigers used to live all over Asia. Today, the Caspian, Bali and Javan tigers are extinct. The Chinese, Siberian and Sumatran tigers are endangered. Like tamarins, tigers are losing their forest habitat. Tigers are also endangered because hunters kill them for their bones and skins.

Siberian tiger

Tiger skins are used to make rugs and coats. Tiger bones are pounded into powder and used to make pills. Some people think the pills will help them to stay young. Even though scientists say the pills do not help, many tigers are killed to make these pills.

African elephant and calf

⊂⊃   African **elephants** are the largest animals on land, but their size does not protect them from the possibility of becoming extinct. Because of their huge size, elephants have to eat a lot and they often travel for miles each day looking for trees, leaves, and plants to eat. As people build more and more roads and cities, it makes it hard for the elephants to travel safely and find food.

Elephants are also killed for their ivory **tusks**. People take the ivory and carve it into ornaments and bracelets.

African elephants

The **elephant's tusks** are big teeth. The elephants use their tusks and their trunks to rip up trees so they can eat them. Sometimes they rip up farms and crops, too. This makes the farmers angry, so they kill the elephants. The elephants do not know they are taking people's food. They are just hungry and want to eat.

Red wolf

The red wolf used to roam all over the southeastern part of America. People built farms, roads and houses and the wolves had less habitat. The wolves began hunting on farms, eating the farmers' cows and chickens. The farmers began to kill the wolves. By 1980, almost all red wolves had been killed. They were almost extinct. They now live only in zoos and **protected** parks, called **reserves**.

Brown bear mother and cub

 **Protected** parks and **reserves** help save animal habitats. Animals that live in these parks cannot be killed. There aren't any farms there, just forest, grass, lakes, and streams.

This funny looking animal is called a **manatee**. Some **manatees** live in the sea and the rivers of Florida. They are gentle and shy and eat sea grass. A long time ago, sailors thought **manatees** were mermaids! Like many sea animals, **manatees** may be dying out because water pollution is drastically changing their habitat.

Manatee and diver

Another reason manatees are endangered is that too many people drive their boats very fast through the water. **Manatees** often swim slowly near the surface of the water. Boats crash into them and hurt them. Some manatees are hurt so badly, they die.

Humpback whale

Humpback whales are another endangered sea animal. They are some of the biggest animals on the planet, but they are also graceful and gentle. They live in big herds. They eat fish. They sing and whistle in the water. People used to go out in boats and hunt whales. Whale fat—called blubber—can be used to make lipstick, paint and wax. So many whales were hunted and killed, they became endangered.

Humpback whale

Today people make wax and paint from other things besides whale blubber. New laws have saved many whales from becoming extinct. Each year, there are more whales in the water.

Polar bear and cub

Polar bears are large white bears that live in the **Arctic**, near the North Pole. They dig tunnels in the snow to make their dens in which they sleep. They have big claws to help them dig. Their claws also help them hunt seals to eat. They hunt in the summer. Then they go in their dens and **hibernate** through the snowy winter. "**Hibernation**" is like sleeping, but it is for a long, long time.

Polar bear family

 **Polar** bears walk far out on the **arctic** ice to hunt. Their white fur helps them hide on top of the ice so they can catch seals that come out of the water. Polar bears have to eat a lot of seals before they can **hibernate**. They need to get very fat before they sleep for such a long time. Like you, polar bears do not eat while they are sleeping!

Polar bear

Polar bears are endangered for many reasons. They are hunted for their fur. Oil spills make the ocean dirty and the bears can get sick.

Recently, polar bears have been dying because they cannot hunt enough seals before winter. The ice around the North Pole is melting because of **global warming**. **Global warming** means that the sea, air and land all over the world are getting much warmer.

Polar bear

In the Arctic the air is so cold that the ice gets very thick and hard. Polar bears walk on the ice to hunt, but **global warming** has made a lot of the ice melt, get thin, and crack. Polar bears are so big and heavy that they cannot walk on the thin ice. They do not catch as many seals. They do not get fat before they hibernate and some of them die.

Factory smokestacks

⌭⌭ Smoke and pollution from burning coal, car engines and factories are some of the causes of global warming.

When we burn coal for heat or gasoline to make our cars run, the engines give off waste gases in the same way a fireplace gives off smoke. These gases are sometimes called **greenhouse gases**, because they float in the sky where they trap heat on Earth instead of letting it escape into outer space. This makes the air much warmer everywhere in the world.

 Lots of **greenhouse gas** comes from cars. If people drove their cars less often, global warming might slow down.

Trees can also help slow global warming. Trees soak up some of the greenhouse gas and help put clean, fresh air into the sky.

Fruit bat

There are over 950 different species of bats all over the world. Many of them are endangered because of human's use of **pesticides**.

Pesticides are special chemicals that are **usually** used to kill bugs and other pests, but they can also **poison** the animals that eat bugs, like bats and birds.

Bald eagle

 Bald eagles do not **usually** eat bugs, but pesticides can still hurt them. Bald eagles sometimes eat the mice and fish that have been **poisoned** by **pesticides**. Some years ago, bald eagles were endangered because of this.

Bald eagle nest

Pesticides made the eagles lay eggs that had thin, weak shells. The eggs broke before the baby eagles were ready to hatch. In some places, there weren't any baby eagles for many years.

It took a long time for scientists to figure out that bald eagles were endangered because of pesticides. Once they figured out the problem, people acted quickly. Some of the most harmful pesticides were **outlawed** in the United States. People stopped spraying them on crops and trees.

Bald eagle

Farmers have not used the **outlawed** pesticides that hurt eagles and their eggs for many years. Now the eagles are no longer as endangered as they once were. There are more and more eagles born every year. The babies grow up. They fly in the air, over the mountains and rivers. They hunt in fields and streams. Bald eagles have been saved.

Polar bear with cubs

Animals, people, and plants are all **connected,** but sometimes it's hard to see how driving a big car, which puts out lots of greenhouse gas, connects with polar bears hunting very far away. It's hard to remember that using pesticides in your yard can hurt an eagle hunting high up in the air, or a whale swimming in the ocean.

Freeway traffic

   The more you remember how animals, people and plants are **connected**, the more you can help save endangered species.

There are many things people can do to save animals from becoming extinct. Habitat loss, global warming and pollution are all problems you can help to solve at home.

Planting a tree

Saving energy and **recycling** are ways to help endangered animals. Saving energy slows down global warming. You can save energy if you turn off the lights, computer and TV in your house when you are not using them. You can turn the heat down in the winter and wear a sweater. Walk, ride your bike, or take a bus instead of a car. Plant a tree. All these actions help reduce greenhouse gases.

Logged timberland

Paper is made from trees, so **recycling** paper saves
forests. Before you throw away paper, see if you can
use it again. Use both the front and the back of your
paper. Then take used paper to a recycling center where
it can be made into new paper. This will help save
forest habitats all over the world—and saving forest
habitats will help save animals.

Raccoon drinking from a stream

Remember that pesticides contain poisons that can hurt animals, so use them with care. Pesticides can wash into streams and creeks and pollute the ocean. Careful use and disposal of pesticides and other harmful chemicals, like paint and engine oil, can help save fish, birds and animals everywhere. Don't dump these toxic items in the street drains or down your sink. Even little actions can make a big **difference** if we all take part.

The world is a home to people, plants, and animals. We share the water, land and air. If you remember we are all connected, you can help save endangered animals. You can make a **difference**. You can help keep the world safe for all living things.

If you liked
***Endangered Animals,* here are two other**
***We Both Read*® Books you are sure to enjoy!**

Explore the mystery and wonder of the tropical rain forest! Travel around the equator to Africa, Asia, and South America discovering the world's most fascinating plant and animal life. Captivating photographs, along with compelling text, make this Level 1–2 book an exciting adventure and a great learning experience.